Twenty to Make

Tiaras &
Hairpins

Michelle Bungay

Search Press

First published in Great Britain 2008

Search Press Limited
Wellwood, North Farm Road,
Tunbridge Wells, Kent TN2 3DR

Reprinted 2009, 2010, 2011, 2012

Text copyright © Michelle Bungay 2008

Photographs by Debbie Patterson,
Search Press Studios

Photographs and design copyright
© Search Press Ltd 2008

Print ISBN: 978-1-84448-327-3
Epub ISBN: 978-1-78126-006-7
Mobi ISBN: 978-1-78126-061-6
PDF ISBN: 978-1-78126-115-6

Suppliers
If you have difficulty in obtaining any of the
materials and equipment mentioned in this book,
then please visit the Search Press website for
details of suppliers: www.searchpress.com

Printed in Malaysia

*Dedicated to my family:
thank you for all your
love and support.*

Contents

Introduction

I could never have imagined that making hairpins for my own wedding would start me off on a new and interesting career. Years later, sitting in my jewellery studio on the edge of Sherwood Forest, putting a book together on the subject of tiaras and hairpins has given me a wonderful opportunity to reflect on the path these creations have taken me down.

Tiaras are traditionally worn by brides on their wedding day, but many of the designs in this book are a twist on the classic shape expected of a tiara, and could easily be worn by a wedding guest instead of a hat. Each tiara has a matching hairpin, so they can be worn by bridesmaids to complement the bride's tiara, but many of the hairpin designs are suitable for all kinds of special occasions and the colour combinations are endless. I've found that plastic-tipped wavy hairgrips or bun pins are ideal for the hairpin designs in this book.

Most of the tiaras in this book incorporate a wire-twisting technique. It takes practice, but once you've mastered it you will find that you can create many interesting shapes and styles.

I hope you'll gain a great deal of satisfaction from making these designs. The crystals are lovely to work with and the end results are very special; watching friends walk down the aisle wearing tiaras I have made has been a highlight for me, and I hope you also get the opportunity to see one of your tiaras worn by a bride on her wedding day.

Michelle

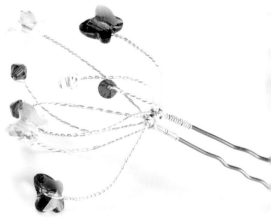

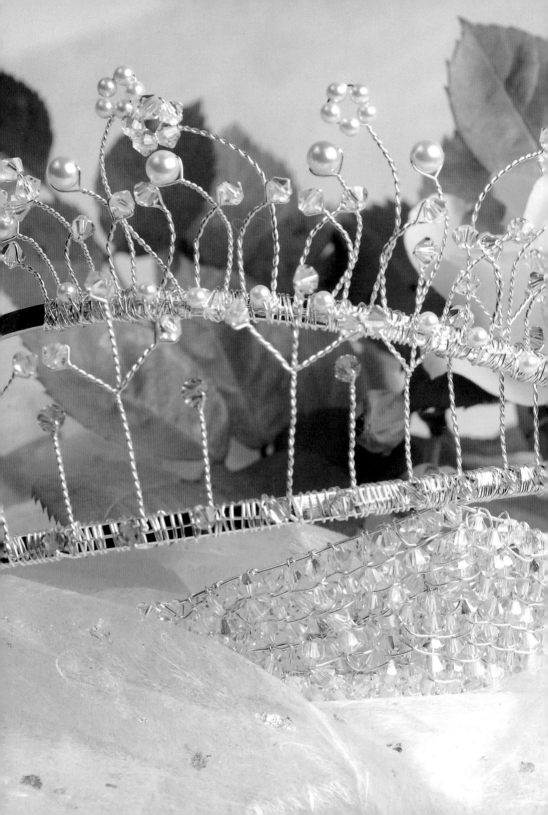

Whatever style you are looking for, there is bound to be a design in this book that will excite and inspire you. All the designs can be adapted simply by changing the types and colours of the beads you use, making this book a treasure trove of ideas and inspiration!

Meadow

Tiara

Materials:

37 x 4mm clear crystal beads
9 x 4mm freshwater or faux pearls
7 x potato-shaped pearls
Silver-plated tiara band
0.4mm silver-plated wire

Tools:

Round-nosed pliers
Flat-nosed pliers
Side-cutter pliers
Jeweller's ring clamp (optional)

Instructions:

1 Cut a 60cm (23½in) length of wire, thread a bead into the centre of the wire and bend the ends down.

2 Hold the bead between your fingers (or in a ring clamp). Using round-nosed pliers, hold the two strands of wire about 3cm (1¼in) away from the bead. Keep the pliers still and twist the bead until the two lengths of wire are twisted tightly together.

3 Bend the excess wires outwards and repeat the process using a variety of beads until you have approximately thirty-five strands of varying length, each one 5mm (¼in) apart. Reserve sufficient crystals to decorate the front of the tiara band. Make the outer strands shorter so that the tiara is highest at the front and tapers down each side. Leave at least 5cm (2in) of wire at each end.

4 Starting from the centre of the tiara band, attach the strands by wrapping the excess wire tightly around it, using the flat-nosed pliers to flatten the wire to the band.

5 Decorate the front of the tiara band by threading crystals on to a 100cm (39½in) length of wire at regular intervals as you wrap it around the band, taking it around the band several times at each end.

6 Finally, bend each of the strands in different directions to create the meadow effect.

Hairpin

Use the same technique to create a pretty, contrasting hair accessory to match a lilac dress.

Hearts

Tiara

Materials:

9 x 4mm clear crystal beads
16 x 4mm blue crystal beads
6 x blue crystal heart beads
Silver-plated tiara band
0.4mm silver-plated wire

Tools:

Round-nosed pliers
Flat-nosed pliers
Side-cutter pliers
Jeweller's ring clamp (optional)

Instructions:

1 Cut a 60cm (23½in) length of wire, thread a heart bead into the centre of the wire and bend the ends down.

2 Hold the bead between your fingers and hold the two strands of wire about 2cm (¾in) away from the bead with the round-nosed pliers. Hold the pliers still and twist the bead until the two lengths of wire are twisted tightly together to form a stem.

3 Bend the excess wires outwards and continue adding alternate clear and heart beads in the same way until you have created a row of twisted stems approximately 1cm (½in). Leave at least 5cm (2in) of wire at each end.

4 Repeat the process until you have a total of fifteen heart and clear crystal strands.

5 Starting from the centre of the tiara band, attach the strands by wrapping the excess wire tightly around it, using the flat-nosed pliers to flatten the wire to the band.

6 Decorate the front of the tiara band by wrapping an 80cm (31½in) length of wire around it, threading blue beads on to the wire as you pass it between the strands. Secure it by wrapping the excess wire around the band several times at each end.

7 Gently bend each strand to finish off the design.

Hairpin

Pink hearts on a hairpin make a good alternative for adult bridesmaids. These look lovely in a group of three in pinned-up hair.

Wire Lily

Tiara

Materials:
7 x 4mm black crystal beads
Silver-plated tiara band
0.4mm silver-plated wire
0.6mm silver-plated wire
6 x silver-plated crimp beads

Tools:
Round-nosed pliers
Flat-nosed pliers
Side-cutter pliers
Jeweller's ring clamp (optional)

Instructions:
1 First make the four centre stamen for the lily. Take a 60cm (23½in) length of 0.4mm wire, thread a bead into the centre of the wire and bend the ends down.

2 Twist the bead, making a strand approximately 3cm (1¼in) long, and repeat the process to make a total of four strands.

3 The flower itself is made from one long piece of wire. Cut a 100cm (39½in) length of 0.6mm wire and loop the wire into a petal shape, twisting it at the base of the petal. Make another loop and twist the wire in the centre, creating a figure-of-eight shape. Repeat this process to form five petals.

4 Thread the centre stamen through the flower and, with the excess wires, wrap the flower tightly to the side of the tiara band. Use the flat-nosed pliers to flatten the wire to the band.

5 Create the three extra strands using 0.6mm wire. Wrap them on to the tiara band with a crystal at one end, squeezed tightly between two crimp beads.

6 Finally, shape the ends of the petals into the classic lily shape using round-nosed pliers. Gently bend the stamen and petals for a more natural look.

Hairpin

With dusky pink centre crystals, this hairpin would be ideal for a wedding guest or ladies' day at the races, as a striking alternative to a feather hair accessory or hat.

Crystal Lily

Tiara

Materials:
154 x 4mm clear crystal beads
Gold-plated tiara band
0.4mm gold-plated wire
0.6mm gold-plated wire

Tools:
Round-nosed pliers
Flat-nosed pliers
Side-cutter pliers
Jeweller's ring clamp (optional)

Instructions:
1 First make the flower. Cut a 100cm (39½in) length of 0.6mm wire, thread on thirty beads and bend the beaded section of wire into a petal shape, twisting the wires together at the base. Thread on another thirty beads, make a second loop and twist the wires in the centre, creating a figure-of-eight shape. Repeat this process to form five petals.

2 Make the four centre stamen. Take a 70cm (27½in) length of 0.4mm wire, thread it through the wire in the centre of the flower, thread on a bead and twist to make a strand approximately 3cm (1¼in) long. Wrap the wire round the centre of the flower and continue the process to make four stamen.

3 Use all the excess wire to wrap the flower tightly to the side of the tiara band, using the flat-nosed pliers to flatten the wire to the band.

4 Finally, bend the stamen and petals into the classic lily shape.

Hairpin

This striking fuchsia pink alternative is wired on to a hairpin and would complement pink oriental lilies in a bride's bouquet.

Grecian Pearls

Tiara

Materials:

16 x potato-shaped freshwater
   pearls

10 x 4mm pale gold crystal beads

Gold-plated tiara band

0.4mm gold-plated wire

Tools:

Flat-nosed pliers

Side-cutter pliers

Instructions:

1 First cut a 100cm (39½in) length
of wire and bend one end so that
the beads do not slide off. Thread on a
crystal, followed by two pearls and then a
crystal. Repeat until all the beads are on
the wire.

2 To secure the beads to the band, wrap the longer, bare end of
the wire around the band, passing it between the beads to hold
them tightly in place.

3 Secure the excess wire at each end by wrapping it tightly
around the band and flattening it using the flat-nosed pliers.

Hairpin

This subtle tiara can be enhanced with lots of single pearl and
crystal pins, making a simple but effective hair decoration.

Fireworks

Tiara

Materials:
27 x 4mm clear crystal beads
Silver-plated tiara band
0.4mm silver-plated wire

Tools:
Round-nosed pliers
Flat-nosed pliers
Side-cutter pliers
Jeweller's ring clamp (optional)

Instructions:
1 Cut a 60cm (23½in) length of wire, thread a bead into the centre of the wire and bend the ends down.

2 Hold the bead between your fingers, and grasp the two strands of wire about 2cm (¾in) away from the bead using round-nosed pliers. Keep the pliers still and twist the bead until the two lengths of wire are twisted tightly together to form a strand.

3 Thread on another bead and twist a further 3cm (1¼in) of wire to create a longer strand.

4 Bend the excess wires outwards and continue adding beads in the same way until you have created approximately fifteen strands of varying lengths (the shorter ones with only one bead). Leave at least 5cm (2in) of wire at each end.

5 Group the strands together and wrap them tightly on to the side of a tiara band using the excess wire. Flatten the excess wire to the band using flat-nosed pliers.

6 Fan out the strands and bend each one into a slight arc to create the firework effect.

Hairpin

Scaling down the size and adding black crystals creates a subtle hairpin alternative to this flamboyant tiara.

Tiara

Materials:

74 x 4mm clear crystal beads
Silver-plated tiara band
0.4mm silver-plated wire

Tools:

Round-nosed pliers
Flat-nosed pliers
Side-cutter pliers
Jeweller's ring clamp (optional)

Instructions:

1 Cut a 60cm (23½in) length of wire, thread a bead into the centre of the wire and bend the ends down.

2 Hold the bead between your fingers and use round-nosed pliers to hold the two strands of wire about 4cm (1½in) away from the bead. Hold the pliers still and twist the bead until the two lengths of wire are twisted tightly together.

3 Bend the excess wires outwards and continue adding beads in the same way until you have created a row of approximately thirty-three twisted stems 5mm (¼in) apart, leaving at least 5cm (2in) of wire at each end. Make the outer strands slightly shorter so that the tiara is highest at the front and tapers down each side.

4 Starting from the centre of the tiara band, attach the strands by wrapping the excess wire tightly around the band. Use the flat-nosed pliers to flatten the wire to the band.

5 Decorate the front of the tiara band by threading all the remaining crystals on to a 100cm (39½in) length of wire and securing it by wrapping the excess wire around the band. Pass the wire between each crystal and take it around the band several times at each end.

6 Bend each strand into a zig-zag shape using flat-nosed pliers.

Hairpin

This contemporary hairpin design can be worn on its own or scattered around pinned-up hair. The subtle colour would complement a pretty pink bouquet.

Butterfly

Tiara

Materials:
72 x 4mm clear crystal beads
4 x silver-plated crimp beads
2 x 3mm faux pearls
Silver-plated tiara band
0.6mm silver-plated wire
0.4mm silver-plated wire

Tools:
Round-nosed pliers
Flat-nosed pliers
Side-cutter pliers

Instructions:
1 For the large wings, thread twenty
crystal beads on to a 60cm (23½in) length of
0.6mm wire and bend the beaded section into
a loop, twisting the wires together at the base. Thread
another twenty beads on to make a second loop and twist the
wires in the centre.

2 Repeat this process using sixteen crystal beads for each of the
smaller wings.

3 Wrap the excess wire around the centre of the wings to form
the butterfly's body and pass the two ends of the wire up behind
the butterfly to form the antennae.

4 Cut the antennae to approximately 4cm (1½in) and thread a
crimp bead, pearl and another crimp bead on to the end of each
one. Squeeze the crimp beads with flat-nosed pliers to
secure them.

5 Finally, using 0.4mm wire, attach the butterfly to the side
of a tiara band and bend the wings and antennae upwards to
resemble a butterfly.

Hairpin

This hairpin was created as a more adult alternative to the tiara.
Use 4mm beads and pretty, clear and pink crystal butterflies.

Leaves and Sparkle

Tiara

Materials:
Silver-lined crystal Delica beads
Silver-plated tiara band
0.4mm silver-plated wire

Tools:
Round-nosed pliers
Flat-nosed pliers
Side-cutter pliers
Jeweller's ring clamp (optional)

Instructions:
1 Cut a 60cm (23½in) length of wire, thread approximately twenty beads into the centre of the wire and bend the beaded section round into a small leaf shape.

2 Hold the beaded leaf shape between your fingers or in a ring clamp and clasp the two strands of wire about 2cm (¾in) away from the bead in the round-nosed pliers. Hold the pliers still and twist the leaf shape until the two lengths of wire are twisted tightly together.

3 Bend the excess wires outwards and continue adding beads in the same way until you have created a row of approximately fifteen twisted stems 1cm (½in) apart, leaving at least 5cm (2in) of wire at each end. Make the outer strands slightly shorter so that the tiara is highest at the front and tapers down each side.

4 Starting from the centre of the tiara band, attach the strands by wrapping the excess wire tightly around it, using the flat-nosed pliers to flatten the wire to the band.

5 Decorate the front of the tiara band by wrapping an 80cm (31½in) length of wire around the band, threading beads on to the wire as you pass it between the strands. Secure it by wrapping the excess wire around the band several times at each end.

6 Gently bend each leaf to complete the design.

Hairpin

This simple design lends itself well to this gold-plated wire hairpin. Several could be worn together to create a stunning effect.

Spiral Fizz

Tiara

Materials:
70 x 4mm dark red crystal beads
Gold-plated tiara band
0.4mm brass-plated wire

Tools:
Round-nosed pliers
Flat-nosed pliers
Side-cutter pliers
Jeweller's ring clamp (optional)
Cocktail stick

Instructions:

1 Cut a 60cm (23½in) length of wire, thread a bead into the centre of the wire and bend the ends down.

2 Hold the bead between your fingers and hold the two strands of wire about 3cm (1¼in) away from the bead using the round-nosed pliers. Hold the pliers still and twist the bead until the two lengths of wire are twisted tightly together.

3 Bend the excess wires outwards and continue adding beads in the same way until you have created a row of approximately twenty-seven twisted stems 5mm (¼in) apart, leaving at least 5cm (2in) of wire at each end. Make the outside strands slightly shorter so that the tiara is highest at the front and tapers down each side.

4 Starting from the centre of the tiara band, attach the strands by wrapping the excess wire tightly around the band. Use the flat-nosed pliers to flatten the wire.

5 Decorate the front of the tiara band by threading all the remaining crystals on to a 100cm (39½in) length of wire and securing it by wrapping the excess wire around the band. Pass the wire between each crystal and take it around the band several times at each end.

6 Finally, wrap each strand around a cocktail stick, and carefully pull out the cocktail stick to create the corkscrew effect.

Hairpin

These spiral hairpins look lovely worn in curly hair, and the pale blue and gold colour of the beads provides a good sparkly contrast to the silver wire.

Bramble

Tiara

Materials:

70 amethyst and rose quartz stone chip beads

Silver-plated tiara band

0.4mm silver-plated wire

Tools:

Round-nosed pliers

Flat-nosed pliers

Side-cutter pliers

Jeweller's ring clamp (optional)

Instructions:

1 Cut a 60cm (23½in) length of wire, thread a bead into the centre of the wire and bend the ends down.

2 Hold the bead between your fingers and, using the round-nosed pliers, hold the two strands of wire about 1.5cm (¾in) away from the bead. Hold the pliers still and twist the bead until the two lengths of wire are twisted tightly together.

3 Bend the excess wires outwards and continue adding beads in the same way until you have created a row of approximately thirty-eight twisted stems of various lengths, about 5mm (¼in) apart, leaving at least 5cm (2in) of wire at each end. Make the outer strands slightly shorter so that the tiara is highest at the front and tapers down each side.

4 Starting from the centre of the tiara band, attach the strands by wrapping the excess wire tightly around it. Use the flat-nosed pliers to flatten the wire to the band.

5 Decorate the front of the tiara band by wrapping an 80cm (31½in) length of wire around it, threading beads on to the wire as you pass it between the strands. Secure it by wrapping the excess wire around the band several times at each end.

6 Finally, bend each strand using flat-nosed pliers to create the messy bramble effect.

Hairpin

These lovely, creamy green amazonite stone chips give an interesting and earthy look to this hairpin.

Flower Garden

Tiara

Materials:

35 x 3mm faux pearls
9 x 5mm faux pearls
39 x 4mm crystal beads
Silver-plated tiara band
0.4mm silver-plated wire

Tools:

Round-nosed pliers
Flat-nosed pliers
Side-cutter pliers
Jeweller's ring clamp (optional)

Instructions:

1 Cut a 60cm (23½in) length of wire, thread five small pearls into the centre and bend the ends down. Wrap them into a circle to create a tiny, abstract flower.

2 Hold the beads between your fingers and use the round-nosed pliers to hold the two strands of wire about 3cm (1¼in) away from the bead. Hold the pliers still and twist the bead until the two lengths of wire are twisted tightly together.

3 Bend the excess wires outwards and continue in the same way until you have created a row consisting of eight flowers made of both pearls and crystals; nine strands topped with a single large pearl; and nineteen strands of various lengths, each with a single crystal at its tip. The strands should be approximately 5mm (¼in) apart, leaving at least 5cm (2in) of wire at each end.

4 Starting from the centre of the tiara band, attach the strands by wrapping the excess wire tightly around it. Use the flat-nosed pliers to flatten the wire to the band.

5 Decorate the front of the tiara band by wrapping an 80cm (31½in) length of wire around the band, threading small beads on to the wire as you pass it between the strands. Secure it by wrapping the excess wire around the band several times at each end.

6 Gently bend the strands in different directions to complete the design.

Hairpin

Use gold-plated wire and rich, red crystals teamed with pearls to complement a deep red dress or a bouquet of red roses.

Woodland

Tiara

Materials:
18 x 4mm clear crystal beads
24 x 4mm pink crystal beads
Silver-plated tiara bands
0.4mm silver-plated wire

Tools:
Round-nosed pliers
Flat-nosed pliers
Side-cutter pliers
Jeweller's ring clamp (optional)

Instructions:
1 Cut a 60cm (23½in) length of wire, thread a bead into the centre and bend the ends down.

2 Hold the bead between your fingers and hold the two strands of wire about 1cm (½in) away from the bead using the round-nosed pliers. Hold the pliers still and twist the bead until the two lengths of wire are twisted tightly together.

3 Bend the excess wires outwards, add a bead to create another branch on each side and twist. Continue adding beads in the same way until you have created a row of six tree shapes and nine straight strands, approximately 1cm (½in) apart, topped with a single pink bead. Leave at least 5cm (2in) of wire at each end.

4 Starting from the centre of the tiara band, attach the strands by wrapping the excess wire tightly around it. Use the flat-nosed pliers to flatten the wire to the band.

5 Decorate the front of the tiara band by wrapping an 80cm (31½in) length of wire around the band, threading beads on to the wire as you pass it between the strands. Secure it by wrapping the excess wire around the band several times at each end.

Hairpin

A wintery, antique look can be achieved by using brass-plated wire and clear crystals to create the hairpin.

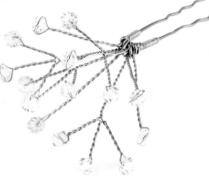

Snow Queen

Tiara

Materials:

37 x 4mm clear crystal beads
22 x 4mm freshwater pearls
Silver-plated tiara band
0.4mm silver-plated wire

Tools:

Round-nosed pliers
Flat-nosed pliers
Side-cutter pliers
Jeweller's ring clamp (optional)

Instructions:

1 Cut a 60cm (23½in) length of
wire, thread a bead or a pearl into
the centre of the wire and bend the
ends down.

2 Hold the bead between your fingers and,
using the round-nosed pliers, hold the two strands
of wire about 2cm (¾in) away from the bead. Hold the
pliers still and twist the bead or pearl until the two lengths of
wire are twisted tightly together.

3 Bend the excess wires outwards and continue adding beads
and pearls in the same way until you have created a row of
approximately thirty-three twisted stems of the same length
5mm (¼in) apart. Leave at least 5cm (2in) of wire at each end.

4 Starting from the centre of the tiara band, attach the strands
by wrapping the excess wire tightly around it. Use the flat-nosed
pliers to flatten the wires to the band.

5 Bend the strands in different directions, keeping the strands
straight to give a spiky effect.

6 Decorate the centre of the tiara band by wrapping an 80cm
(31½in) length of wire around the band, threading beads and
pearls on to the wire as you pass it between the strands. Secure
it by wrapping the excess wire around the band several times at
each end.

Hairpin

Brass-plated wire and pale gold crystal beads teamed with
pearls give this hairpin a simple sophisticated look.

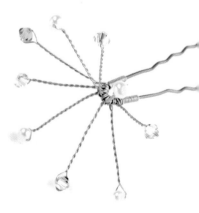

34

Sweeping Strands

Tiara

Materials:

12 x 4mm dark pink crystal beads
12 x 5mm faux pearls
24 silver-plated crimp beads
Silver-plated tiara band
0.6mm silver-plated wire

Tools:

Flat-nosed pliers
Side-cutter pliers

Instructions:

1 Find the middle of a 12cm (4¾in) length of wire and wrap it tightly around the centre of the tiara band several times to create two ends of wire of equal length.

2 Bend the wires apart to create a V-shape. Thread a crimp bead on to one of the wires, followed by a pearl, a crystal and another crimp bead, then close the crimp beads with flat-nosed pliers, trimming off the excess wire.

3 Repeat the process, spacing the wires approximately 4cm (1½in) apart.

4 Bend each strand so that they overlap to create the crown shape.

Hairpin

Experiment with different colour combinations. This hairpin has pretty lilac and dark purple crystals which catch the light.

Oak Leaf

Tiara

Materials:

4 x 4mm freshwater pearls
Gold-plated tiara band
0.4mm gold-plated wire
0.6mm gold-plated wire

Tools:

Flat-nosed pliers
Round-nosed pliers
Side-cutter pliers

Instructions:

1 Start at the top of a leaf. Cut a length of 0.6mm wire approximately 40cm (15¾in) long and bend it in the centre using round-nosed pliers to form the tip of the leaf.

2 Bend both wires outwards approximately 1.5cm (¾in) down the wire. Bend them back down using round-nosed pliers to create the first two points to the leaf.

3 Continue until the oak-leaf shape is complete and twist the wires together at the bottom of the leaf.

4 Create the central leaf vein with a separate piece of wire, wrapping one end around the top of the leaf and the other around the base.

5 Make a second leaf and use the excess wire to secure the leaves tightly to the tiara band.

6 Wrap 0.4mm wire around the bottom of the leaves. As you do so, thread on the pearls to form a cluster. Bend the leaves back to finish off the design and create a realistic leaf shape.

Hairpin

This larger version on a hairpin is finished off with dark red crystals. This design would really suit an autumn-themed wedding.

Gypsophila

Tiara

Materials:

48 x misshapen pearl beads
31 x 4mm pearl beads
Silver-plated tiara band
0.6mm silver-plated wire
96 x silver-plated crimp beads

Tools:

Round-nosed pliers
Flat-nosed pliers
Side-cutter pliers

Instructions:

1 Starting from the centre of the tiara band, wrap lengths of wire tightly around the band at 1cm (½in) intervals. Use 3.5cm (1½in) strands at the centre of the band and shorter strands at the sides. Create twenty-two strands altogether.

2 Thread a misshapen pearl on to each strand between two crimp beads and squeeze the crimp beads tightly using flat-nosed pliers to secure them. Add one pearl to each of the shortest strands, and two or three to the longer ones.

3 Decorate the front of the tiara band by wrapping an 80cm (31½in) length of wire around the band, threading round pearl beads on to the wire as you pass it between the strands. Secure the wire by wrapping the excess around the band several times at each end.

4 Gently bend each strand of wire in different directions to complete the design.

Hairpin

This hairpin has slightly longer stems and works well with gold-plated wire.

Catherine Wheel

Tiara

Materials:

10 x 4mm pink crystal beads
5 x 4mm clear crystal beads
Silver-plated tiara band
0.4mm silver-plated wire

Tools:

Round-nosed pliers
Flat-nosed pliers
Side-cutter pliers
Jeweller's ring clamp (optional)

Instructions:

1 Cut a 30cm (11¾in) length of wire, thread a bead into the centre of the wire and bend the ends down.

2 Hold the bead between your fingers and hold the two strands of wire about 3cm (1¼in) away from the bead using the round-nosed pliers. Hold the pliers still and twist the bead until the two lengths of wire are twisted tightly together.

3 Bend the excess wires outwards and continue adding beads in the same way until you have created four short rows of twisted stems, with three or four strands in each row. Include a row of slightly shorter strands approximately 1.5cm (¾in) long.

4 Gather all the strands together in a group and wrap them tightly on to one side of the tiara band.

5 Finish the tiara by fanning all the strands out then gently bending them in the same direction, bringing the shorter strands to the centre to create the swirl design.

Hairpin

These striking dark purple beads work well against the silver wire. Imagine five of these arranged all around elaborately pinned-up hair.

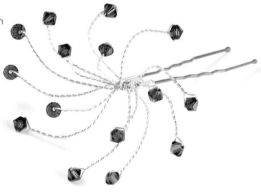

Tiara

Materials:

115 x 4mm purple crystal beads
35 x 4mm clear crystal beads
Silver-plated tiara band
0.6mm silver-plated wire

Tools:

Flat-nosed pliers
Side-cutter pliers

Instructions:

1 Cut a 15cm (6in) length of wire
and wrap the middle tightly around
one side of the tiara band two or
three times. Secure the wires together
with a twist on the top of the band and
leave the excess wire pointing outwards.

2 Cut a further two lengths of wire and wrap them
around the first to create the five points of a star.

3 Repeat the process to create two further wire stars, one each
side of the first.

4 Thread ten purple crystals on to each strand of the two outer
stars, and three purple followed by seven clear crystal beads on
to each strand of the star in the middle. Create a small loop at
the top of each strand with the round-nosed pliers to secure the
crystals in place.

5 Finally, bend the crystal strands into shape.

Hairpin

This design has a wintery feel to it. Use deep red
crystals against the icy clear ones for a Christmas wedding.

Ice Cluster

Tiara

Materials:
180 x 4mm clear crystal beads
Silver-plated tiara band
0.4mm silver-plated wire
0.6mm silver-plated wire

Tools:
Flat-nosed pliers
Side-cutter pliers

Instructions:

1. Start by making a frame on the tiara band, which the crystals can be wrapped around. To do this cut a 50cm (19¾in) length of 0.6mm wire, bend the wire in the middle and, with the point approximately 3cm (1¼in) above the centre of the tiara band, secure the ends of the wire to the band to make an inverted V-shape.

2. Create a second layer for the frame, just below the first, and secure it tightly at each end to the tiara band.

3. Using long lengths of 0.4mm wire and starting on one side of the tiara, start wrapping the wire around the frame, threading crystals on to the front and passing the wire through gaps over and between the beads as you go.

4. Keep threading beads on tightly together and secure the ends of all the excess wires by wrapping them through the mass of beads, hiding the ends by cutting them as close as possible to the tiara.

Hairpin

Pearls were included in this design along with a few small, twisted strands to add some more dimension.

Acknowledgements

Thanks to Sky Blue Designs for the use of all materials and equipment used in the book.

www.skybluedesigns.co.uk

Publishers' Note

If you would like more books on making beaded jewellery and other items, try the following Search Press books:

Necklaces, Bracelets, Brooches and Rings using Crystal Beads and *Crystal Beaded Jewellery* by Christine and Sylvie Hooghe, 2006

Designs for Beaded Jewellery Using Glass Beads by Maria Di Spirito, 2006

The Encyclopedia of Beading Techniques by Sara Withers and Stephanie Burnham, 2005